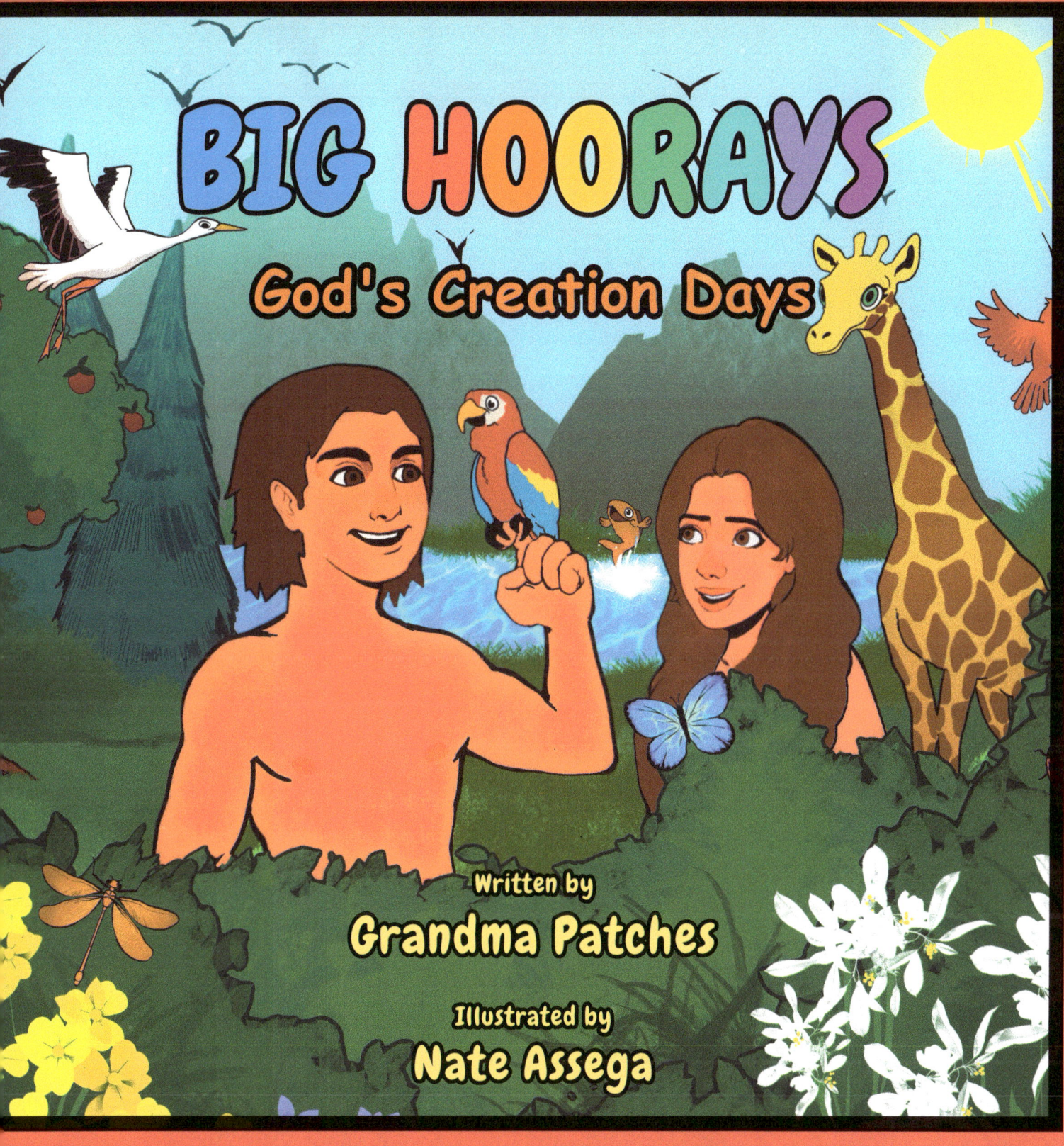

Copyright © 2024 Grandma Patches. All rights reserved.

All rights reserved. No part of this publication may be reproduced, distributed, or transmitted in any form or by any means, including photocopying, recording, or other electronic or mechanical methods, without the prior written permission of the publisher, except in the case of brief quotations embodied in critical reviews and certain other noncommercial uses permitted by copyright law.

ISBN Paperback: 979-8-89316-317-9
ISBN Hardback: 979-8-89316-316-2
ISBN ebook: 979-8-89316-318-6

Dedication

I dedicate this book to God the creator of all things, who has given me, the least of his servants, eternal life through his son, Jesus/Yeshua.

To my parents, who without you there would be no me. I have not forgotten you, and I thank God for both of you. May you rest in peace, and, by God's mercy, may we meet again.

To my husband, who encouraged me to make this book and the series that is unfolding. Your patience and support through this process has brought this book into being. I love you!

To my eleven children, from the oldest down to my youngest, you each hold a special place in my heart. I love and appreciate each one of you.

To those who are married in, I love seeing how you compliment my children and what God is doing in each of the new family units God is creating through you. Each one is a gift from heaven.

To my grandchildren who are a continual joy to your grandpa and me as we grow older. You help remind us how we are to be before God, coming to him as a little child.

To all people, who the Bible says "were created" in the image of God. This truth gives each person a special calling on their life. May this book help reinforce that calling to walk in God's image at a young age.

A Little Note of Encouragement

It is never too early to instill the love of praise to the God of heaven and earth into the hearts and minds of our children. These rhymes were inspired from Genesis 1 and 2:1-3. May you enjoy this special time together praising God with your little ones.

BIG HOORAYS
God's Creation Days

Written by
Grandma Patches

Illustrated by
Nate Assega

Did you know at the whole world's start,
In the beginning, when it was dark,

God spoke and there was light?
HE divided day from night.

BIG HOORAYS
God's Creation Days

Written by
Grandma Patches

Illustrated by
Nate Assega

Did you know at the whole world's start,
In the beginning, when it was dark,

God spoke and there was light?
HE divided day from night.

This was when the world had begun,
And so ended day number one.

Let's praise God for this great day!
Let's give God a big, Hooray!

Did you know God spoke into place,
An area to put some space?

There was water that needed to go,
Above this space and down below.

That was all God wanted to do,
And so ended day number two.

Let's praise God for this great day!
Let's give God a big, Hooray!

God made plants and each tall tree,
And so ended day number three.

Let's praise God for this great day!
Let's give God a big, Hooray!

Did you know God made each star?
HE put them up there really far.

HE spoke and made the moon and sun,
HE made the heavens so much fun!

These lights in space we all adore,
And so ended day number four.

Let's praise God for this great day!
Let's give God a big, Hooray!

So many animals came alive,
And so ended day number five!

Let's praise God for this great day!
Let's give God a big, Hooray!

Did you know God made weird bugs,
All creepy-crawlies, ants, and slugs?

Humans completed God's wonderful mix,
And so ended day number six.

Let's praise God for this great day!
Let's give God a big, Hooray!

Did you know that when HE was done,
God finished all HE had begun?

Seven days were the right amount.
Are you ready? Let's all count...

One, two, three, four, five, six, SEVEN!
Let's worship our great God in heaven!

Let's praise God for all these days!
Let's give God SEVEN big Hoorays!

HOORAY! HOORAY!
HOORAY! HOORAY!
HOORAY! HOORAY!
HOORAY! HOORAY!

Dear Readers and Friends,

    Did you like praising God for each creation day? There are more engaging activities about Creation at grandmapatches.org where you can download free worksheets to go along with the story.

    Hope to see you there!

                Love,

                Grandma Patches

PS Don't forget to go to Amazon and leave a review so other youngsters can enjoy my stories too!

When Grandma Patches was a little girl, she would often find herself reading the first couple chapters of Genesis from the Bible and ponder the creation story.

After she grew up and became a stay-at-home mom of eleven children, she became rather good at taking hard subjects and making it easier for children to understand. Now a grandmother, she felt inspired to take that skill and teach children about God and HIS story through rhyme.

Grandma Patches hopes to foster a love for God and his word to the next generation. By creating fun and helpful materials, Grandma Patches wants to support parents and grandparents as they bring up their children and grandchildren in the ways of Yehovah.

When Nate Assega was a child, he spent hours reading children's books just like this one. He loved looking at the illustrations and one day decided that he would like to draw pictures too.

After he practiced drawing everything and learning more in school, his pictures became better and better and still improve to this day.

As the illustrator of this book, he hopes to inspire some children, just like he was inspired.

"All you need to do is pick up a pencil."
nmassega@gmail.com

Acknowledgments

To my dear friends (you know who you are) who came beside me and gave me specific, wise counsel as I was putting this story together. I am so grateful for each of you. Your friendship, wisdom, and encouragement throughout this book creating process was so helpful.

To my amazing coach (Brittany Plumeri) and all the people at selfpublishing.com, my talented editor (Glenys Nellist), and my gifted illustrator (Nate Assega) for assisting me through this incredible process of bringing this book to life.

I cherish each person's role in helping to nurture this book along to the place that it can now fly. Thank you!